Young Heroes

KOKODA SUNRISE

Del Merrick
Dion Hamill

RISING STARS

In memory of Arthur Gordon Briggs.
Stolen by war.

First published in the UK by
Rising Stars UK Ltd.
7 Hatchers Mews, Bermondsey Street, London SE1 3GS
www.risingstars-uk.com

This edition published 2011
Reprinted 2015

Text © UC Publishing Pty Ltd.
www.ucpublishing.com

First published 2006 by Insight Publications Pty Ltd.
ABN 57 005 102 983,
89 Wellington Street,
St Kilda, Victoria 3182
Australia

Development: UC Publishing Pty Ltd
Cover design: UC Publishing/Design Ed
Written by: Del Merrick
Illustrations: Dion Hamill
Text design and typesetting: Design Ed/Clive Sutherland
Editorial consultancy: Dee Reid

All rights reserved. No part of this publication may be reproduced, stored in a retrieval system or transmitted in any form by any means, electronic, mechanical, photocopying, recording or otherwise without the prior permission of Rising Stars Ltd.

British Library Cataloguing in Publication Data.
A CIP record for this book is available from the British Library.

ISBN: 978-1-84680-808-1

Printed by Craft Print International Ltd., Singapore

Contents

Introduction 4

The Kokoda Track 5

Chapter 1 Home before dark 7

Chapter 2 Left for dead 12

Chapter 3 Bless the biscuits 17

Chapter 4 Finding the Golden Staircase ... 23

Chapter 5 Who's there? 28

Chapter 6 The camp at Uberi 33

Chapter 7 Mangivar's gift 38

Introduction

During World War II, the Japanese army invaded Papua New Guinea. Australia thought the Japanese would invade them next. So they sent troops to Papua New Guinea.

From July 1942 to January 1943, Australian soldiers fought the Japanese in Papua New Guinea along the Kokoda Track.

Conditions were terrible. The soldiers had to battle the wetness, the knee-deep mud and the difficult terrain of the Owen Stanley Range. All supplies and equipment had to be carried because the track was only passable on foot.

After months of fighting, the Japanese were defeated. Australia was safe from invasion.

But this victory might not have happened without the people of Papua New Guinea. Papuans carried food and supplies to the Australians along the Kokoda Track, as well as wounded soldiers to safety.

The Australian soldiers and their Papuan friends walked down the Kokoda Track and into history.

The Kokoda Track

Characters

Chapter 1
Home before dark

Mangivar hurried along the uneven jungle trail. He had been visiting his grandmother and he was late. Soon it would be dark and his parents would begin to worry.

At fifteen, Mangivar was the eldest boy in his family. Since the death of his grandfather, it was his job to take food to his grandmother. She lived some way away in the mountains.

The mountains were cold at night and the jungle trail was steep and unsafe. Mangivar was not afraid of the dark. But now there were new dangers lying hidden in the jungle.

Recently, war had come to Mangivar's home of Papua. Australian soldiers now marched along the narrow Kokoda Track. They were on the look-out for the invading Japanese army.

The Australian soldiers found life in the jungle very hard. There were steep mountain peaks and deep valleys and rushing streams. It was hot and steamy. The heavy rain turned the ground into slush.

The soldiers kept slipping and falling in the mud. Leeches sucked the blood on their bare legs. In the day it was so hot that sweat dripped from their faces. At night they were cold and wet. They were often hungry and frightened. Their feet and clothes were never dry.

By now, it was night. Dark clouds hid the moon, making it hard to see. Mangivar tried to hurry but it was not easy. The track was just slippery, wet mud. Suddenly, his foot caught on something. He fell hard, hurting his shoulder.

Mangivar lay still. He heard a night bird call. Then he heard a voice. It was so low it could have been mistaken for the wind in the trees.

He listened hard. The words were not clear but he could tell they were Japanese.

Mangivar was scared. He lay still, hardly daring to breathe.

Chapter 2
Left for dead

Then Mangivar heard a moan. He moved around slowly, and reached out. His fingers touched a still body. Mangivar had tripped over a man!

The clouds parted and the moon lit the track for a moment. On the ground was an Australian soldier. In his hand was a machine gun. His eyes were closed and his face was twisted in pain. He didn't look much older than Mangivar himself.

Then the soldier moaned again. Mangivar moved a little closer.

The soldier's eyes opened. 'Who are you?' he asked weakly.

'I'm Mangivar. I live near here,' Mangivar whispered in Pidgin English.

'I'm Private Dyllan Little.' The soldier's voice was just a whisper.

'Where are you hurt?' asked Mangivar.

'My leg. Japanese soldiers ambushed me. They thought they'd killed me.' Pain made Private Little stop for a moment. 'I must warn the other soldiers. They'll be coming up the track.'

Mangivar looked at Private Little. The soldier was in no shape to make it to the Australian camp at Uberi.

'What should I do?' thought Mangivar. There were Japanese soldiers all around. If he went to warn the Australians, his life would be in danger. But if he didn't go, many lives would be in danger.

Mangivar knew that his family would expect him to help Private Little.

'I'll take the message back for you. I'll warn the Australians and bring help back for you.'

Mangivar dragged Private Little off the track and covered him with fern leaves. This would hide him from the Japanese soldiers and keep him a little warmer.

Private Little reached into his pocket. He pulled out an old photo and the stub of a pencil. He wrote some words on the back of the photo and handed it to Mangivar.

'Take this to the camp. They'll know what to do. Good luck, and thanks.'

Chapter 3
Bless the biscuits

Mangivar made his way back along the track, slipping and sliding in the mud. His heart raced. He listened hard to every sound.

The track was steeper now and a mist had fallen. Vines scratched his arms and legs. He shivered in the cold mountain air.

Then Mangivar heard a noise. He was sure it had come from behind him. He edged back into the cover of the ferns off the side of the track.

Suddenly, the ground gave way beneath his feet. He lost his balance and began sliding down the steep mountainside. He snatched at low branches as he slid past, but they broke off in his hands.

He only stopped when his body slammed into something large and soft, wedged against a fallen log.

Mangivar lay very still. Blood trickled from a cut on his head. He waited and listened. Had the enemy heard him? But there was no sound and no one came.

He moved into a sitting position. He looked at what had stopped his fall. It was a large sack.

Mangivar realised it was a supply parcel. Aeroplanes called 'Biscuit Bombers' dropped these parcels for the Australian troops. They had food, clothing, medical supplies and,

sometimes, letters from Australia in them. The planes couldn't always see where to drop the parcels so some landed far away from the camps.

Mangivar cut through the sack. There were tins of baked beans and bully beef, biscuits, bandages, ammunition, thick socks, soap and towels, and a blanket. There was also a bundle of letters for the soldiers written by their families in Australia.

Mangivar pulled on a pair of thick socks and put the blanket round his cold body. He ate some of the sweet biscuits. He started to feel stronger.

Suddenly he heard a burst of gunfire. 'Time to go,' thought Mangivar. 'It's a long way to the camp.'

Mangivar tied the letters and ammunition to his chest with a bandage. He found a large safety pin, and pinned the blanket round his shoulders. Finally, he cut a strong branch to use as a walking stick. He looked sadly at the supplies on the ground. He would have to leave them behind. He had no way of carrying them.

Chapter 4
Finding the Golden Staircase

The climb back to the track was very slow. The moon had disappeared behind the clouds. Mangivar could barely see. He had to feel his way through the thick jungle with his hands.

But worse than the darkness was the fear. Mangivar was afraid of making any noise, afraid of the Japanese and afraid of falling again. Most of all, he was afraid of letting Private Little down.

'What if I don't make it?' he thought. 'Will the Australian soldiers walk into an ambush?'

Mangivar knew he had to get help so he kept on climbing. He lost track of time. His head throbbed. His knees ached. But Mangivar kept on going. 'The soldier, he needs me,' he thought over and over again. 'Must get help.

Slowly, he crawled his way back up the mountain.

At last, he reached the track. Ahead of him was a high ridge. Mangivar knew he would have to climb it. Would he have the strength? 'Just keep going,' he told himself. 'One foot after the other.'

He climbed on and on, up and up. By the time he reached the top, Mangivar was exhausted.

'I'm nearly there,' thought Mangivar. He gathered every last bit of strength and made his way to the 'Golden Staircase'. This was the thousand steps that the Australian soldiers had built to climb up and down the steep ridge. These steps would lead him down to the Australian camp at Uberi.

The steps were narrow and slippery. Mangivar thought they would never end. He worried about Private Little. Was he still hidden and safe? Or was he dead? Mangivar was so exhausted, but he kept on going. Private Little was depending on him.

It took him over an hour to reach the last step. His knees gave way under him and he fell to the ground. He looked up. It was almost sunrise.

'Don't you worry, Private Little. I'll soon be there,' he whispered. 'Your message will be delivered.'

He rose to his feet and began to walk the final part.

Chapter 5
Who's there?

Suddenly, Mangivar froze. He had sensed a slight movement behind him. Was it a possum? Or a cassowary? He wasn't sure. He hid behind some low bushes. Then he heard a sound—the sound of breathing.

Mangivar held his breath. Fear gripped him. The sound came closer and closer, then it stopped. Would he be seen? He stayed as still as a statue.

Suddenly, Mangivar felt a sharp prod in his back. 'Get up!' a voice ordered in a fierce whisper.

'That's an Australian voice!' Mangivar thought. He pulled the old photo from his bag. He held it over his shoulder so the man behind him could see it clearly.

Mangivar felt the rifle move away from his back. 'OK, get up and turn around,' the Australian ordered in a kinder voice.

Mangivar stood up and turned around to face him. The Australian soldier was a big, strong man. He looked hard at Mangivar and he kept the rifle pointed at him.

'Where did you get that photo?' the soldier asked.

Mangivar's heart beat fast and his legs trembled, but he held his head high. 'Look on the other side,' he said.

The soldier turned the photograph over and read the message. He looked at Mangivar in amazement.

'You brought this message so far? And at night? Well done, mate, well done!' He shook Mangivar's hand. Then he put his rifle over one shoulder, and placed a hand on Mangivar's arm.

'What's your name, young man?'

'Mangivar, sir.'

'Are you hungry, Mangivar?' he asked, smiling.

'Yes, sir, I'm starving,' said Mangivar, smiling back.

'Then let's go and eat!'

Chapter 6
The camp at Uberi

The two moved off down the track to the Australian camp.

Mangivar felt he had done well.

'I kept my promise to Private Little,' Mangivar thought. 'The Australian soldiers will be warned.'

But when he saw the soldiers, Mangivar did not feel so good. They sat huddled under thin grey blankets, drinking tea and eating stale biscuits. They were silent and just stared into the distance.

'I wish I could have brought the rest of the parcel,' he thought. 'Everyone looks so exhausted and unhappy.'

As Mangivar and the soldier came closer, the men jumped to attention. 'Good morning, men,' said the Captain.

'Good morning, Captain Briggs, sir,' they replied, raising their hands in salute.

Mangivar watched as Captain Briggs told his men about Private Little and his message.

'We can't leave him up there, alone and wounded,' said the captain. 'I need volunteers for a rescue mission.'

Mangivar jumped up.

'Wait! I've got something to give you,' he said.

The soldiers looked at him in a bored way.

'Look!'

Mangivar threw back the grey blanket and showed them the bandage tied around his chest. He slit the bandage with his sharp knife. Letters and ammunition spilled to the ground.

There was a stunned silence.

Then a soldier ran forward and picked up the letters and held them in the air. The soldiers let out a cheer. They waited as the letters were passed around, everyone hoping for a letter from home.

Chapter 7
Mangivar's gift

The soldiers were thrilled. The letters made them feel that they were not alone, that they were not forgotten.

Now, the men were talking and laughing. Captain Briggs found some bully beef, sugar and flour. He cooked some food to have with tins of hot, black tea.

The food cheered the men up. They were a lot happier than when Mangivar first saw them.

Captain Briggs sat with Mangivar on the steps of a wooden hut. They sipped tea and ate the food. Captain Briggs watched his men as they re-read their letters, laughing and sharing their news.

'This is the best gift you could have given them,' he said. He turned to thank Mangivar, then smiled. Mangivar had fallen asleep against his arm.

'Sleep while you can, Mangivar,' he said quietly. 'You'll need your strength for the rescue of Private Little.'